MW00423533

PRAISE FOR ROOTED

"*Rooted* is a great primer on the basics of Christian theology–presented in a way that is fresh, accessible, and concise. A great introduction for new believers and a great refresher for those who need to remember why the gospel really is good news."

Trevin Wax – Managing Editor of *The Gospel Project* and Author of *Gospel-Centered Teaching*, *Counterfeit Gospels*, and *Clear Winter Nights*

"Medders and Smith get it–we're all theologians, but we're not always clear. So they wrote a short book to make it simple. You have in mind right now people who need to grow in doctrine, and you now have in your hand a tool to help them. Buy *Rooted* and read it; then get a copy for them too!"

Dave Harvey – Pastor, Author, Executive Director of Sojourn Network, and Blogger at AmIcalled.com

"It has been said that theology is like a skeleton. It is essential for providing support and structure to the body, but if it's the only thing visible, then the body is either malnourished or dead. Theology as it's presented in *Rooted* is the furthest thing from malnourished or dead. This book attempts, quite successfully I believe, to steer the imagination toward a truth that catches fire, a system that fosters life, and a faith that expresses itself in love.

Scott Sauls – Senior Pastor of Christ Presbyterian Church in Nashville, TN and Author of *Jesus Outside the Lines*

"The moment you say or think anything about God, you're doing theology. Satan knows more theology than you, but he hates what he knows. And he hates seeing you forget about yourself to gaze on your God. In *Rooted*, Medders and Smith take us by the hand to show us not just theology's importance, but its beauty. Best of all, you can hear them worshiping as they write. I pray you'll worship as you read."

Matt Smethurst – Managing Editor of The Gospel Coalition

"Some books we read for pure pleasure. Other books are resources, tools to shape our minds and hearts. This is the latter. Smith and Medders have put together a concise, foundational, accessible book to introduce a reader to the study of theology. It's almost a defense of theology, which is necessary in our day of self-defined truth and loose handling of Scripture. *Rooted* is an ideal little book for group study and discussion or for personal benefit. Church leaders should keep a few close at hand to help hungry, curious congregants with their questions."

Barnabas Piper – Author and Podcaster

"What a delightful little book! Our hearts love God no further than our minds know him, yet sadly, theology is too often done for the theologians instead of for the rest of us. This book, though, is rich in truth yet accessible to all. It will awaken anyone who gives it a chance to the joy of studying what matters most in life."

Dane Ortlund – Executive Vice President and Bible Publisher at Crossway and Author of *Edwards on the Christian Life*

"Smith and Medders have written a manifesto for Christians everywhere to grow in right understanding and worship of God. This is a very enjoyable read, and a powerfully important book that will build up your faith."

Matt Brown – Author of *Awakening* and Founder of Think Eternity

ROOTED:

THEOLOGY FOR GROWING CHRISTIANS

J. A. Medders
& Brandon D. Smith

Rooted: Theology for Growing Christians
© 2016 by J. A. Medders and Brandon D. Smith

All rights reserved.

Published by Rainer Publishing
www.rainerpublishing.com

ISBN ISBN 978-0692623053

Printed in the United States of America

Scripture quotations are from the ESV® Bible (The
Holy Bible, English Standard Version®), copyright ©
2001 by Crossway, a publishing ministry of Good News
Publishers. Used by permission. All rights reserved.

To Natalie and Christa, our wonderful wives who never let us forget the gospel and who endlessly encourage our ministries for the bride of Christ.

TABLE OF CONTENTS

ACKNOWLEDGEMENTS

From Jeff

I'm grateful for every faithful Christian who has opened God's Word and told me what it means. I want to thank all of the people who taught me in Sunday school, from kindergarten to high school, sowing theological seeds, watering, pruning, refining, and encouraging me to know and love God. I'm thankful for Pastor Richard Caldwell and his faithful preaching. I'm grateful for Paul Helbig, my first and favorite professor in Bible college, who modeled and invited me to the thrill of knowing and loving the triune God. I'm thankful for John Piper's call to glorify God by enjoying God. Many thanks to Wayne Grudem, whose readable *Systematic Theology* was like a magic carpet ride to a whole new world of knowing and loving God.

I'm grateful for my dear wife, Natalie, and her cheering me on to write. I'm thankful for the wonderful saints at Redeemer Church who remind me how theology is for life in Christ. I'm thankful for my co-author's kindness, friendship, and encouragement. Most of all, all glory, honor, praise, and thanksgiving to the Father, Son, and Holy Spirit. May the words of this book and the meditation of my heart be acceptable in your sight.

From Brandon

Writing a book is no small endeavor, and there are numerous people who have played an important role in this work.

I'm grateful, first and foremost, to my wonderful wife, Christa. She is my best friend and God's greatest earthly gift to me. I'm immensely thankful for my co-author's contribution to this book, for it is far better with him than without him. My deepest gratitude to the students, staff, and faculty at Criswell College who invested in me and impacted me in various ways in my Criswell career as a student, staff member, and professor. Most of this book was dreamed up and written while they sharpened and encouraged me. Many thanks to Trevin Wax, Malcolm Yarnell, Jared Wilson, Owen Strachan, Everett Berry, Steve Timmis, Jason Duesing, Micah Fries, Barnabas Piper, Alvin Reid, and Michael Cooper for their feedback at various stages of this project, which began incubating almost four years ago.

I'm grateful most of all to the triune God, who called, saved, and sealed me. Because of his grace, I'm not who I was and am not yet who I will be.

FOREWORD

I'm afraid many people think of theology the way they think of chess. They know it takes skill and intelligence. Maybe they wish they were smart enough to play chess, but, then again, they really wouldn't want to be part of the high school chess club. Theology seems, to them, to be dry, dusty, complicated, and disconnected from life—maybe even disconnected from the spiritual disciplines of being a Christian. If that's you, or if you know people who feel this way (and you do), this book will help you.

Rooted is a book by and for those who want to know why theology matters. It's also a book that recognizes that the church has often worked hard to make theology bloodless and boring—exactly the opposite of the riveting, exhilarating, life-giving truths revealed to us by God.

Brandon Smith and J. A. Medders get this. That's why they've written this brief primer on theology. Don't worry. This isn't the equivalent of reading a complex manual on the quantum mechanics of the script of a science fiction movie you once saw. This book starts with the premise that knowing God, and knowing God's point of view on the cosmos as revealed in his Word, is for every Christian, not just for those who seem "wired" to enjoy speculative and complex discussions.

Moreover, this book assumes what I've found to be true: that theology disconnected from mission becomes archaic, abstract, and boring. It's not that we don't believe in justification *sola fide* or in the ordo salutis or in the hypostatic union—even those who aren't sure what those words mean. We just often have trouble seeing how those old words and ideas are supposed to actually help us in our fight against sin, in the evangelism of our children, or in our advocacy for widows and orphans.

Theology separated from mission—that is, separated from the life that Jesus has called us to live in him—is not biblical theology. Christ Jesus said that his sheep hear his voice, and they run toward it. Hearing the voice of Christ makes us move. This is because theology isn't ultimately about a "what" but about a "Who." Theology is to show us how God patterned the universe after Jesus Christ, how he is summing up all things in Christ, how in Christ he as put together a plan to reconcile humanity to God and to one another, thus freeing the whole universe to be what it was created to be as the theater of God's glory.

This book is not for readers who want to play theologian for a few hours. As the title implies, it's for Christians who want to grow. The kind of theology in this book is the kind of theology you need when your children are rebelling, when your marriage is in trouble, when a new abortion clinic comes to town, or when a tyrant throws you into prison. Theology matters because theology is about Jesus Christ. And Jesus Christ is the ground and future of the universe. My prayer as you read is that you would not only learn, but that you would long, not just for a way of life or for a set of truths, but for the Way, the Truth, and the Life.

Russell Moore

President, The Ethics & Religious Liberty Commission

INTRODUCTION:
WHY STUDY THEOLOGY?

L et's do a little mental exercise. What is the first thing that comes to mind when you see these next three letters crammed together? G-o-d.

What rises to the surface as you think about God? Do you think about his goodness? Maybe you think about how God is love (1 John 4:8), or that he is three-times holy (Isa. 6:14). But did you think about his wrath? Maybe not—if not, why not? Did you only think about the Father, or did you also consider that Jesus and the Spirit are both God?

When we hear someone's name, we think of their character and their accomplishments. When you see

"Tiger Woods," you will think, "Golfer." And you might also remember some of the deep problems in his personal life and character. So when you read "God," did you happen to think about any of the mighty acts of God? Creation? The Flood? The parting of the Red Sea? Did the Incarnation pop up? Did you think about God the Son, the New Adam, born of a virgin, living a sinless life, dying on that Roman torture device, in your place, for your sins, and rising again?

WHAT IS THEOLOGY?

All of the words you've read so far are theology. The word "theology," at its most basic definition, means "words about God." We are all theologians. While there are a select few on planet earth who get paid to be theologians, the truth is that all humans are in some respects a theologian—we all have thoughts of God, and they are either right or wrong. Theology is all about God: all God is, all he has done, all he does, and all he will do. And the task of theology is that we would speak of God rightly, truthfully, and worshipfully. Theology isn't simply for the mind—it's for life. We are to speak the right things about God, and we are to live rightly for God, that we may worship him in spirit and in truth (John 4:23–24). Theology matters because worship matters. God's glory matters, and therefore, how we worship God matters. This is why, as A.W. Tozer said, "What comes into our minds when we think about God is the most important thing about us."[1]

God likes to be worshiped in a particular way. More pointedly, there is a way that God demands to be worshiped. In Job 42:7, God gets angry with Job's buddies because they didn't speak rightly about God. "My anger burns against you and against your two friends, for you have not spoken of me what is right, as my servant Job has" (Job 42:7). While Job was suffering, his friends said all kinds of wrong things about God to him. They believed in God, but had wonky theology, and it touched down in the real moments of life.

Good theology is always practical. Christians should never say, "Theology schmeology." Theology is not a museum of collected data about God, but according to C. S. Lewis, "Theology is a lot like a map." How so? Think about how maps were made two hundred years ago. Someone went on a journey, chronicled what they saw, drew contours, elevation, coastlines, etc.—and they did this to help others navigate the location. Theology is a map for us sojourners. "Doctrines are not God: they are only a kind of map. But that map is based on the experiences of hundreds of people who really were in touch with God."[2]

The aim of theology is worship: meeting with God, living with God, and living for God. We aren't studying some inanimate object in theology; we are beholding the living God. Theology is for the adventure of life with God. What could be more practical? Your theology is never secluded in the attic of your life; it saturates all areas of life. God wants to be worshiped for who he is, not for who we think he might be. Ask Job's buddies.

So, how's your theology? Are you lazy towards theology? Resolve, right now in this moment, no longer to treat theology like a professional sport for pastors and professors. Theology is a part of following Christ, who is, according to John 1:1–14, the God (Greek: *theos*) who is also the Word (Greek: *logos*). Jesus is the Truth (John 14:6); he is theology in the flesh, theology with ten fingers and ten toes. And we worship him truthfully, evangelize with truth, live in a community of truth—this is theology, life in Christ. "The purpose of doctrine," Kevin Vanhoozer says, "is to ensure that those who bear Christ's name walk in Christ's way. Far from being irrelevant to 'life,' then, doctrine gives shape to life."[3] Since Jesus is the Way, the Truth, and the Life (John 14:6), theology's aim is live according to his way, his truth, and his life—that we are following rather than opposing Jesus of Nazareth.[4]

THE GOSPEL REVEALS THEOLOGY

For Christians, theology is helping us answer the question, "How should we live?"

This includes everything: thinking, feeling, and doing. Christian theology is to inform our lives because, "I have been crucified with Christ. It is no longer I who live, but Christ who lives in me. And the life I now live in the flesh I live by faith in the Son of God, who loved me and gave himself for me" (Gal. 2:20). We are gospel people. We are the crucified. Theology is anchored in Christ and therefore extremely gospel-driven.

What is the gospel, you ask? It's a beautiful, powerful, life-giving truth. It is, literally in the Greek, "good news." Paul gives us a glimpse of this good news: "For I delivered to you as of first importance what I also received: that Christ died for our sins in accordance with the Scriptures, that he was buried, that he was raised on the third day in accordance with the Scriptures" (1 Cor. 15:3–4). As the Bible tells us, Jesus was crucified, buried, and rose again. He has come to rescue creation from the jaws of death. This is *of first importance.* The gospel really is that simple. But in its simplicity, the gospel is profound. As we will see, the truth of the gospel is easy enough for even a child to understand, yet it has a massive, far-reaching impact on every nook and cranny of our lives. That may sound a little intrusive, but it is the best news you will ever hear.

Our theology should be centered on this glorious gospel, for without it, we do not have Christian theology. If Christ is not our center, we've lost what it means to be Christian. The word "Christian" literally means "little Christ." The gospel is our theology and from it the rest of Christian theology flows. The Apostle Paul told the Corinthians, "For I decided to know nothing among you except Jesus Christ and him crucified" (1 Cor. 2:2). This doesn't mean he taught them nothing but the gospel—it means he taught them everything in relation to the gospel. You cannot experience, or know, any doctrine until you've experienced the gospel. When the cross becomes more than a blood-encrusted log to becoming your life and your all, the meaning of the universe opens up to you. There are 10,000 "Aha!" moments when you look at this world through the gospel. "For by Jesus all things were created, in heaven and on earth, visible and invisible, whether thrones or dominions or rulers or authorities—all things were created through him and for him. And he is before all things, and in him all things hold together" (Col. 1:16–17). You can't believe *that* until you've believed the gospel.

We must always remember that the gospel points to Jesus. The gospel in a very real sense *is* Jesus. We have the clearest picture of God in God the Son. "No one has ever seen God; the only God, who is at the Father's side, he has made him known" (John 1:18). As Michael Bird says, "the gospel is the nexus into the reality of the God who has revealed himself."[5] Want to know about God? Want to know who he is and what he does? Look to Jesus in the Scriptures.

As we will see, the gospel is wrapped up in the Trinity—Father, Son, and Holy Spirit. They all play an equally vital part in salvation. But you cannot think about the gospel fully until you've beheld the glory of God in the face of Jesus. When you see the gospel, you see Jesus. When you see Jesus, you see God. When you see God, you see the truth. And as Jesus says, the truth will set us free (John 8:32).

THEOLOGY IN OUR HEARTS AND MINDS

Jesus was once asked, what is the greatest commandment? Jesus replied that it is two-fold. First, "You shall love the Lord your God with all your heart and with all your soul and with all your mind" (Matt. 22:37). We often get the heart and soul part,

29

but do you love God with all your *mind*? We usually don't struggle with whether or not to love God with our hearts or even our souls, but do you love God with your *mind*? God wants you to know him on every level. It is not wrong to "give your heart and soul to God," but he wants your mind, too. He wants you to think rightly about him so that you feel rightly about him. He wants you to know facts about him so that you can have a deeper relationship with him. We are not saved by knowledge of God alone; in fact, even demons know and believe that God exists (James 2:19). We are not saved by theology of the movie *Avatar*, believing that God is a glowing tree, either. The heart, soul, and mind are not separated. God wants it all, together, forever. Through the gospel, good theology brings them together into a fully-formed, rightly-motivated worship of the God of the universe.

Second, Jesus said that "you shall love your neighbor as yourself" (Matt. 22:39). Theology doesn't stop with you because the gospel doesn't stop with you. God is a God of salvation, of rec-onciliation. Paul was unashamed of the gospel because "it is the power of God for salvation to everyone who believes, to the Jew first and also to the Greek" (Rom. 1:16-17).

The gospel is for everyone. So when Jesus calls us to make disciples of all nations (Matt. 28:19), he wants us to take his truth to them. "How then will they call on him in whom they have not believed? And how are they to believe in him of whom they have never heard? And how are they to hear with-out someone preaching? And how are they to preach unless they are sent? As it is written, 'How beautiful are the feet of those who preach the good news!'" (Rom. 10:14-15). He doesn't simply want you to have good theology; he wants all people every-where to have good theology. As his disciples who are called to make more disciples, it is important for us to tell people about him in a proper way. We don't want them just to know *about* God, but to know God as he has revealed himself.

Good theology is the system of roots that keeps our tree of faith vibrant and alive. It keeps us grounded, centered, and yet growing. When we are rooted, we won't remain stagnant.

WHAT'S NEXT?

David Clark once said that good theology "names and describes the God who is Ultimate Good and who transforms people for good."[6] We believe this. So we wrote this book for you. We want to serve the student, the new believer, the long-time church member, the struggling saint, the weary pastor, the first-time seeker, and the militant atheist. And if these descriptions don't describe you, we want to serve you too. Theology does not belong solely in the seminary classroom; it belongs in the pew and in the living room, in the workplace and in the prison, in the street and in the pasture.

In this book, we will cover some of the most crucial and basic issues in theology. First, we will discuss the Trinity. What does it mean for God to be three-in-one? How do we describe the indescribable union of God the Father, God the Son, and God the Holy Spirit?

Next, we will talk about the Bible. Yes, that heavy, old book that spends more time on people's nightstands than in their hands. How has it lasted for thousands of years? Can we trust what it says?

Then, we will take a look at what happened when the first humans, Adam and Eve, disobeyed God. How did one wrong choice set all of human history into chaos? More importantly, how does Jesus fix this problem and what does it mean for us?

Finally, we will consider the question that everyone asks: What happens when we die and why does life matter now? Television and movies talk of flying babies in diapers and ghosts haunting families. Is that all we have to look forward to? There must be more, right?

Sit back and relax. Read this book slowly and prayerfully. And if you need to read it again, then do so. Let the deep things of God ignite a fire in your heart and mind. Let theology be the compass that points true north, leading you on a journey toward the transformative reality of God's truth.

DISCUSSION AND REFLECTION:

1. What was your feeling about theology before reading this chapter?
2. How does studying theology impact our understanding of the gospel?
3. In what way does theology change our personal devotion to God?
4. How does theology drive you toward sharing the gospel with others?

1
THE GOD WHO IS THERE: THE TRINITY

Everyone loves a hero. We love reports of good Samaritans in our cities, and we love the supernatural, larger than life superheroes. Whether a mild-mannered reporter, who's actually from another planet, or a troubled billionaire try-and-be-a-do-gooder, we are captivated by superheroes—and so are our wallets. The summer of 2012 gave us three major superhero movies: *The Avengers*, *The Dark Knight Rises*, and *The Amazing Spider-Man*. These blockbusters combined to gross over $1.3 billion (yes, billion) in theatres, and launched a multibillion dollar sequence of spin-offs and sequels.[7] Movie critics raved over the notable "believability" of the characters as they showed courageous acts of sacrifice and bravery. Fans of all demographics, often dressed as the superheroes themselves, literally stood and cheered as the credits rolled in theatres across the world. And have you ever thought about why we respond that way? As superheroes fly across the screen, there is something in the human heart that aches, groans, and longs to be caught up and fixated on something bigger than the life we know on this earth.

The popularity of these blockbusters reveals the feet-sweeping effects of nobility, bravery, sacrifice, power, and raw heroism. We want heroes—we *need* heroes, like Gotham needs Batman, or Metropolis needs Superman. We dare to dream that there is still ultimate good in the universe, and we're looking everywhere for it.

You can look right at the Bible and find the

greatest Hero of heroes, the triune God. The Father, the Son, and the Holy Spirit are the greatest alliance of heroes in the universe. They are united on a mission to kill the great enemy Satan, to save the bride of Christ, and to establish the happily ever after of the kingdom of God. The hero of humanity's story is God.

GOD: THREE-IN-ONE

When people think of God, they might imagine an unsocial, distant being that set time and space in motion, then laid down to take a galactic nap. He doesn't care about what happens in our daily lives. He is detached, uninterested, and relatively unpleasant if bothered. He's like a cranky old man who doesn't want you walking on his lawn. You're Dennis the Menace and he's Mr. Wilson. That's not the God of the Bible.

Many Christians will typically think of a Heavenly Father who is pushing buttons, juggling all kinds of cosmic activities, and intervening when necessary. Yes, God is our Father who governs all things and intervenes in our lives, but he is considerably more than the man behind the curtain. In fact, he *must* be more.

Throughout church history, the doctrine of the Trinity (from the Latin word *trinitas*, meaning "the number three") has been held in high regard as one of the primary, essential standards of the Christian faith. But why? The opening sentence of *Our Triune God* by Philip Ryken and Michael LeFebvre correctly states, "To know God is to know him as triune."[8] Though Scripture does not use the word "Trinity," there is no other way to understand God as he truly is.

Here's a humble attempt to explain the Trinity, an eternal wonder, in a nutshell. There is one God who exists in three persons: Father, Son, and Holy Spirit. Each person is fully God, working in perfect relationship with one another, eternally possessing the same divine substance. All three are simultaneously and equally omnipotent (all-powerful), omniscient (all-knowing), omnipresent (everywhere at all times), holy, loving, just, and all other attributes of God. We cannot elevate his one-ness over his three-ness. We cannot elevate his three-ness over his oneness. We cannot elevate one of the Persons over another. They are not set on a better-than-the-other totem pole; they are connected and dependent upon one another. He is three. He is one.

Easy enough, right?

Okay, let's be honest... comprehending the Trinity is a colossal task. This is why some have attempted to describe the Trinity using everyday illustrations. For example, you may have heard that the Trinity is like a stream, a snowflake, and an ice cube: same substance, different forms. These are indeed of same substance, but they don't work together in unison to accomplish the same task. Others might compare God's tri-unity to a sim-

41

ple triangle: three sides, one shape. However, any side taken away immediately makes it no longer a triangle at all, and no side is a triangle by itself. These help us grasp the Trinity in a way, but cannot fully explain it.

It's more helpful, then, to acknowledge that no illustration is sufficient. All analogies, in the end, fail to fully explain God's triune nature. So, we must primarily approach studying the Trinity in sheer amazement at the wonder of God, accepting that he has not chosen to reveal every intricate detail to us. As we try and think about the three-and-oneness of God and the gears in your brain begin to grind, let's respond like the Apostle Paul: "Oh, the depth of the riches and wisdom and knowledge of God! How unsearchable are his judgments and how inscrutable his ways!" (Rom. 11:33). When it comes to the study of God, we go skydiving and deep sea diving into head-scratching, soul-stirring awesomeness.

A MYSTERY MADE KNOWN

The Trinity is a great mystery in many ways, but we can't say that God has hidden this truth from us. Scripture abounds with references to his triune nature. The list of biblical references could fill up this chapter, but let's explore a few instances in which the Father, Son, and Holy Spirit are shown as equal.

John 3:16 says that Jesus, the Son, is "begotten," meaning that he is literally *of* the Father. The Son is not an ordinary created being; he and the Father share the same nature. Jesus isn't some kind of watered-down version of God. He isn't the pre-algebra standard of Godness. Jesus is full on, high-octane God. In John 8:58, Jesus calls himself "I AM." This is the same name that the Father used for himself when speaking with Moses in Exodus 3:13-14. In Mark 3:28-29, Jesus says that blasphemy (denial or cursing) of the Holy Spirit is an eternal and unforgivable sin; just as the Father revealed was a sin against him in the Third Commandment. And when Peter rebukes a man for lying to the Holy Spirit, he emphatically says, "You lied to God" (Acts 5:3-4). The Father is God. The Son is God. The Spirit is God.

The Trinity is explicitly involved in two foundational events in the life and ministry of Jesus, as well. First, at his baptism, Jesus sees the "heavens being torn open and the Holy Spirit descending on him like a dove" while the Father proclaims that Jesus is his Son with whom he is "well pleased" (Mark 1:9-11). Jesus is in the water, the Spirit comes down, and the Father speaks. This event shows the three persons of the Trinity participating in Jesus's mission to restore our broken world, live a perfect life, and forgive sins—acts only God could perform (Mark 2:7-12).

Second, Jesus includes the Trinity in the Great Commission. Prior to his ascension, the resurrected Christ commands his followers to "make disciples of all nations, baptizing them in the name of the Father and of the Son and of the Holy Spirit" (Matt. 28:19). The three persons of the Trinity exercise equal authority over those who place their faith in Christ. They can't and won't be separated. Furthermore, Christ's disciples make more disciples in the name of God: Father, Son, and Holy Spirit. The mission of the church is to spread the gospel of the kingdom of the triune God.

With a basic biblical foundation laid regarding God's three-in-one existence, the vital question now remains: Why can't a person simply worship God without all the extra details?

What is the benefit of delving deeper into the doctrine of the Trinity?

PLUMBING THE DEPTHS

It might be easy to become discouraged by the Mount Everest of studying God, and the aspect of his three-in-one nature in particular. This is understandable. We live in a culture of instant knowledge. Typing a question and finding an answer is as easy as opening an app on a cell phone. Many difficult questions about theology can be found in the same way, however God is more than a search result. A person can't ultimately "Google" him. In light of this, the temptation is to avoid seeking the depths of who he is. It's simply easier to remain, in a sense, unfamiliar with him. Unfortunately, one who settles for such a shallow relationship misses out on the true power of experiencing God as he has revealed himself to us in the Bible.

Imagine two strangers are assigned to the same overnight shift at a warehouse. They are the only two there, five nights a week, stuffing boxes and stocking shelves. At first, they might learn one another's name and share a kind word or two. They'll likely begin to discuss the hot news of the day or some other surface-level topic. Through several weeks and months, they start to discuss their family and share photos of their son's baseball uniform or their daughter's recital dress. Eventually, they talk about the deeper things in life like struggles, doubts, and aspirations. They even discover their shared dream of getting a job with better hours so that they can spend more time with their ever-growing kids.

Over time, they become close friends that can lean on one another, encourage one another, and offer a word of wisdom to one another. Through their time together, they realize that even if one of them did reach that dream of leaving the graveyard shift, their friendship would continue far beyond the warehouse. They are no longer distant strangers; they've become more than just a name to one another.

In a similar yet far more life-altering way, pursuing a deeper connection with God leads to more profound relationship with him. Sin destroys our relationship with God, but from the first instant one places faith in him, it is expected that the bond will be restored and strengthened until the day we die and meet him face-to-face (Phil. 2:12-13; Col. 1:10-14). Besides, he is not merely a co-worker with whom we share a strong bond; he is the Creator of time and space. He is infinitely beautiful, awe-inspiring, majestic, loving, kind, trustworthy, and much more. There is no one who compares to him. We can take our closest relationship in this world, multiply it by several infinities, and still not scratch the surface of what God promises his people. We should dive into the depths of God because we want to know the God who has set his love on us. We want to know him, because he knew us first.

The persons of the Trinity are equal in nature, but distinct in role. Each member of the Trinity has a part to play in the grand story of redemption. So, truly knowing God has vast implications for our daily lives. While we will examine his relationship to his people more closely in later chapters, let us now consider the dynamic community of the triune God.

THE FATHER

The Father is depicted as the catalyst behind the triune God's rescue mission to redeem a people for his glory (Eph. 1:3-6). The greatest example is Jesus willingly submitting to his Father in order to bring about the plan of salvation (Matt. 26:39-42; John 6:37-38). Jesus also promised to send the Holy Spirit—from the Father—to believers (John 14:26; Eph. 1:13-14). Paul testifies that he is the one "from whom are all things and for whom we exist" (1 Cor. 8:6). This means that even as we worship God the Son and God the Spirit, we follow their lead in admiring the Father as the source and object of divine glory.[9]

As the perfect prototype for all earthly fathers, our Heavenly Father demonstrates intense love for his children through discipline, provision, and protection. In Hebrews, the Father's discipline is described as something that he does "for our good, that we may share in his holiness" (Heb.

12:10). James declares that "every good and perfect gift" comes from him (Jam. 1:17). Jesus also promises that the Father will provide everything we need (Matt. 6:25-34) and that no one can snatch believers from his hand (John 10:29). As Bruce Ware explains,

> "[O]n the one hand, God fathers us by calling for our respect and by expecting our obedience. On the other hand, God fathers us by being lavish, generous, even extravagant in his care, love, provision, and protection for his children."[10]

Knowing the Father is a gift in and of itself, but the heaping of such undeserved grace upon believers from the Creator of the universe should astound us. Many people can point to their fathers similarly as inspiring models of leadership, provision, protection, love, sacrifice, and commitment. Indeed, any good father will reflect characteristics of God the Father. But whether a person has a good father, had an older role model to look up to, or has never met their father, our Father in Heaven who created us represents all that a father should be (Ps. 68:3-10). He loved us so much that he willingly sent his own Son into the world to die a gruesome death on a Roman torture device on our behalf to pay for our sins (John 3:16-17).

Believers can know that their Father in heaven is totally capable and worthy of being trusted and worshiped in every aspect of life, and he has earned this right through who he is and what he does for his people. He loves you. Really. His character, and that cross on which the Son died, testify to his unmatchable love. Remember the love of the Father.

THE SON

If Jesus really is God, as we've already established, then we must determine how his eternal role as the Son fits into his life as Jesus of Nazareth–the living, breathing human being who walked the earth for over 30 years. How is he both God and man? And why would he leave the eternal magnificence of heaven to enter time and space as a man?

First, we must acknowledge that Jesus Christ is fully God. In one of the most powerful texts in Scripture, the Apostle John gives an almost poetic account of Jesus's divine nature:

"In the beginning was the Word, and the Word was with God, and the Word was God. He was in the beginning with God. All things were made through him, and without him was not any thing made that was made." (John 1:1-3)

Here, we see Jesus referred to as "the Word" who is God and with God. He is God just as the Father and Spirit are God, yet distinct. Throughout the Old Testament, the words of God were considered perfect, true, and authoritative (Ex. 20:1-21;

Ps. 18:30). The Son, as God, has been there since the beginning and he has been intricately involved in all things (Col. 1:16-17).

Second, we must acknowledge that Jesus Christ is fully human. The Son entered human history, born in Bethlehem, and raised in Galilee as the God-man Jesus Christ to literally and entirely personify the perfect, true, and authoritative words of the triune God. He was a child born of a virgin through the Holy Spirit (Matt. 1:20). Without an earthly father, Jesus did not inherit the sins of Adam and therefore lived the life we were supposed to (Rom. 5:12-21). He came to announce that the Savior had arrived as God had promised (Isa. 7:14; Matt. 1:21-23). His body became a corpse on a cross to pay for sins, and three days later his brain stem kicked back in and he literally rose from the dead to conquer sin and death for us—as he promised (Luke 24:19-26; John 14:1-6; 1 Cor. 15:3, 17).

John says later in his account that "the Word became flesh and dwelt among us" so that we would witness the glory of "the only Son from the Father, full of grace and truth" (John 1:14). As we will discuss later, salvation through Jesus is unfathomably significant for our lives. In the ultimate act of sacrifice, through the most radical mission trip of all-time, God determined long ago that he would redeem all things through the Son (1 Pet. 1:20). And the Son stepping out of the glory of heaven and into our world falls right in line with the mind-blowing blockbuster that is the gospel. This epic story of redemption is not only about individually saving souls; it is about restoring the brokenness introduced by our first parents, Adam and Eve. It is about the brilliance of God radiating in a dull world, now and forever.

The Son brought God's presence to the world in flesh and bones. John tells us, "No one has ever seen God; the only God, who is at the Father's side, he has made him known" (John 1:18). Through Jesus Christ, we are no longer in darkness about who God is and what he expects. We look with confidence to the Word who became flesh, observing the unchanging glory of God and his absolute standard for living. The more like Jesus we become, the more human we really are—the more we walk in the image of God that we've been crafted in. Jesus is the invisible image of God made visible, dressed in flesh and blood, obvious to the naked eye. He is the eternal Son of God, only visible to those who have eyes to see.

THE HOLY SPIRIT

The Holy Spirit is perhaps the most overlooked person of the Trinity in many Christian circles today, but he is equally deserving of the praise and adoration given to the Father and Son. He is the crucial third component to the work of the triune God. The Spirit is the one who introduces us to the Father and Son, and then continues to remind us of the Father and Son.

The name "Holy Spirit" does not give a concrete picture of an individual person like "Father" or "Son" might, but he acts out his distinct role as specifically and uniquely as the other persons. The Spirit isn't an *it*; the Spirit is a *he*. As we discovered earlier, Jesus promised that he would send the Spirit from himself and the Father as a "helper" to live within believers (John 14:16, 26; 15:26; Acts 1:8; Eph. 1:13-14). This promise came true at Pentecost, where the Holy Spirit filled believers and performed miraculous deeds through them (Acts 2:4). Christians experience and represent the triune God through the guidance of the Spirit (John 16:7-8; 1 Cor. 6:19-20; Gal. 5:22-25).

In his book *Forgotten God*, Francis Chan writes, "We are not all we were made to be when everything in our lives and churches can be explained apart from the work and presence of the Spirit of God."[11] It is important to remember that the Holy Spirit literally lives and works in believers (2 Tim. 1:14). Through the Spirit, God himself accompanies Christians through the ups and downs of life, leading us in truth and pointing us toward the joy of knowing him. As if shackles have been undone from our feet, we are liberated by the Spirit to walk in true freedom from the slavery of sin.

The Holy Spirit is not just a mere expression of God, but God himself. Christians should be encouraged to walk in the expectation that we really are empowered to live as children of the Father, being led, as Luke writes, by "the Spirit of Jesus" (Acts 16:7). The Spirit isn't some ooga-booga force; he is the personal presence of God to empower disciples of the risen Jesus to live for the glory of God. This is why Paul can say, "For you did not receive the spirit of slavery to fall back into fear, but you have received the Spirit of adoption as sons, by whom we cry, 'Abba! Father!' The Spirit himself bears witness with our spirit that we are children of God" (Rom. 8:15-16).

ABOVE ALL HEROES

As we've seen, our triune God is a far beyond silver screen victors. No enemy can even land a blow against him, much less defeat him. Superman, Batman, Spider-Man, Iron Man, the Hulk, and every other superhero is pathetic compared to him. The average police officer or firefighter that performs heroic acts is but a shadow next to him. He is the hero of all heroes. In fact, "hero" is a feeble term for such a powerful God. He stands above and beyond all creation, all known wonders of the universe, and all lauded champions the world has ever seen. He created and exercises righteous authority over everything that has existed and will ever exist (Ps. 103:19).

God is more than some sort of cosmic conqueror, ordering his minions to do as he pleases. He cares for his people and does not hide it. In the triune God we have a Father, a Brother, and a Helper. So, not only does his triune nature create absolute wonder in our hearts and minds, but his nearness to us is humbling. The Father has chosen to reveal his love to us through the sacrifice of the Son and the sending of the Holy Spirit (Eph. 1:9-14). As Alister McGrath concludes, "God is both the goal of our journey and the means by which we find him."[12] As you think about God, hear the words of Isaiah, "Behold your God!" (Isa. 40:9). Drink him in. He is the answer to the world's clamoring for something wholly good, for a hero, a hope—he's all that we crave... and so much more.

DISCUSSION AND REFLECTION

1. Before reading this chapter, how would you have described the Trinity? Now that you've read the chapter, did this description change?

2. Why is it important to have a strong grasp of the Trinity?

3. How does understanding the Trinity change our devotion to God?

4. In what way does understanding the Trinity push us to share the gospel with others?

2
THE WORDS OF GOD: SCRIPTURE

The Holy Bible is consistently the best-selling, most-read, and most-quoted book in the entire world. Love it or hate it, you cannot avoid it. Leland Ryken once said that if the Bible ceased to exist tomorrow, the world would not be rid of it: "People passing the gate of Harvard University would continue to read 'open ye the gates that the righteous nation which keepeth the truth may enter in' (Isaiah 26:2). Every year two million visitors would pass the Liberty Bell in Philadelphia and still read, 'Proclaim LIBERTY throughout all the Land unto all the Inhabitants thereof' (Leviticus 25:10)."[13]

In a world where everyone has an opinion about what is true and good, it can be difficult for people to follow the commands of a document containing collections of writings that span over thousands of years. For some, the Bible is filled with good teachings on life, and it should be respected for that, like a relic of human history. For others, the Bible is a giant dust magnet. And many think that the Holy Bible spins the greatest lies ever told—and that would make the book more holey than holy. Everyone has something to say about the Bible. It seems like every generation tries to put the Bible through the ringer. And guess what? The Book is still on the shelves and in our hands.

In 1978, as the debate raged over the Bible's truthfulness, over 200 Christian leaders met in Chicago to draft a statement concerning the Bible's authority. These men put on paper what the Bible has always said about itself: that Scripture was given to human authors through the inspiration of the Holy Spirit and is therefore totally reliable. The opening paragraph of the *Chicago Statement on Biblical Inerrancy* reads:

> *"The authority of Scripture is a key issue for the Christian Church in this and every age. Those who profess faith in Jesus Christ as Lord and Savior are called to show the reality of their discipleship by humbly and faithfully obeying God's written Word. To stray from Scripture in faith or conduct is disloyalty to our Master. Recognition of the total truth and trustworthiness of Holy Scripture is essential to a full grasp and adequate confession of its authority."*[14]

For this group of believers, the ability to rely on Scripture was of such importance that they drafted an extensive testimony to state their case. To them, if the Bible really contains God's words, then it is factual—not opinion, or subject to our opinion—and inerrant (without error), so it must be authoritative in our lives as Christians. We cannot claim to be disciples of Christ and ignore or deny his words. When the Bible speaks, God speaks.

Many Christians would respond to the previous sentence with a hearty "amen!" For a great deal of believers, no explanation is necessary. Just like Paul wrote to our Thessalonian brothers and sisters long ago, "And we also thank God constantly for this, that when you received the word of God, which you heard from us, you accepted it not as the word of men but as what it really is, the word of God, which is at work in you believers" (1 Thess. 2:13). If one accepts the Bible as the words of God, then it should be trusted. End of discussion. (And rightfully so.)

But again, that's not how everyone views the Bible.

Before we go any further, know this: You can trust the Bible because you can trust God's Son.

Jesus of Nazareth prayed for us, to the Father, "Sanctify them in the truth; your word is truth" (John 17:17). What does Jesus say about the Bible? It's true. Ultra-true.

Our God is a gracious and kind God. He has given us reasons *in* the Bible to trust the Bible, and he's also piled up reasons *outside* of the Bible for why we should put our eternal life's savings on what he's revealed to us.

EXTERNAL EVIDENCE FOR TRUSTING SCRIPTURE

"Inerrancy" is a big, fancy word that doesn't get much airtime today. And that's a shame. It's a great word, and helpful if we understand the basic idea of it. Wayne Grudem defines inerrancy as follows: "The inerrancy of Scripture means that Scripture in the original manuscripts does not affirm anything that is contrary to fact."[15] In other words, what the authors recorded with their own pens is true, and the message that it conveys can be trusted. If you could sit down next to the writers as they penned their first manuscript, you would find them meticulously crafting truthful documents.

This is not accepted by everyone, of course. You might hear claims that the Bible has been changed throughout the years—like a group of second graders playing telephone, the message got corrupted and it's no longer credible. Well, there is a wagon-load of evidence to assert the credibility of Scripture. Let's tackle a few highlights about the original manuscripts themselves.

Much can be said about Old Testament texts, but one example currently stands above them all. From 1947-1956, several excavations were performed on the northwest shore of the Dead Sea after a shepherd stumbled upon jars full of ancient manuscripts in an area cave. Of the nearly one thousand texts found, one of the most exciting findings in the Dead Sea Scrolls is referred to as the "Great Isaiah Scroll." Containing the entire text of the Book of Isaiah, this 24-foot long document is the oldest copy of Isaiah known to exist, dated around a thousand years older than the current known manuscripts of the Hebrew Bible.[16] Garry Brantley explains that the Great Isaiah Scroll is "word-for-word identical to our standard Hebrew Bible in more than 95% of the text. The 5% of variation consisted primarily of obvious slips of the pen and spelling alterations." [17] That. Is. Awesome. Can you imagine a 1,000-year-long game of telephone and the message staying intact? Of course not. But God isn't playing a game. He's communicating clearly and directly with his people.

The New Testament texts are equally astounding. Nearly 5,700 known copies of the New Testament exist in the original Greek alone, which is more than double the works of Homer, the second-largest collection that currently exists.[18] All languages included, there are over 24,000 known ancient manuscripts of the New Testament. These manuscripts are remarkably 99.5% consistent with each other, with similarly insignificant differences like those of the Great Isaiah Scroll.[19]

These numbers by themselves are a boost of assurance for us as Christians. The message in the Bible that we read daily hasn't been altered in thousands of years. We don't have to wonder if rogue Christians throughout the years decided to embellish or recreate our faith in order to make it more exciting. We can know historically that God's words say what they mean to say. In fact, Michael Bird points out that recounting Jesus's life and message were crucial to his followers. He argues that Christian communities shortly after Jesus's ascension to heaven were careful to discount and discredit false stories and beliefs about Jesus that circulated among them, adding that "the key task of the early church was to faithfully recall the words and deeds of Jesus."[20] And Jesus didn't just politely ask his followers not to fib on him later, he went a step further—he sent them the Holy Spirit to "teach you all things and bring to your remembrance all that I have said to you" (John 14:26). Here's a brain-buster: God sent God to remind the disciples of what God said when God was among them, and then sent God to remind them of all God said. Go ahead and stick a cotton swab in your ear to clear out the cobwebs.

If Scripture is uncompromised, then we can approach it with the anticipation of learning something true about God. As we will see, the writers were recording the clear revelation of God himself. He communicates through them in written form for our benefit, unveiling his obvious intention to have his people pass along an untainted message from generation to generation. If our God can speak the universe into existence, he can protect the purity of his Word. And evidence seems to show that he's done just that.

THE TESTIMONY OF SCRIPTURE

While there are reasons outside of the words of Scripture to honestly consider its claims, Scripture has much to say about itself. So even if all the science and archaeology in the world disappeared, the Word would still testify about itself.

Its various events, stories, teachings, and letters expose the self-expression of God's unchanging authority. In the words of J. I. Packer, "The scriptural approach to Scripture is thus to regard it as God's written testimony to Himself. ... What Scripture says, He says."[21] It's nearly impossible to read the Bible plainly without being confronted with the fact that God expects you to recognize its words as his words.

The Old Testament bubbles over with phrases that begin with "thus says the Lord." When the prophets began a declaration or teaching with these words, the hearers knew that God was about to talk through that person. Why? They recognized that this was how God had chosen to communicate with them (Amos 3:7). These prophets were not just any Joe off the street who wanted to speak for the Lord; they were God-called people who were empowered by the Spirit (1 Sam. 19:20; 2 Chron. 20:14; Ezek. 11:5), under God's command (Deut. 18:18-22), with accompanying signs or fulfillments that proved their authenticity (1 Sam. 10:3-11; 1 Kings 13:5; 2 Kings 19:29, 20:9; Jer. 28:15-17; Ezek. 33:33).[22] The New Testament teaches this same position when Peter says that "no prophecy of Scripture comes from someone's own interpretation. For no prophecy was ever produced by the will of man, but men spoke from God as they were carried along by the Holy Spirit" (2 Pet. 1:20-21). The words of the Old Testament were then recorded in written form, with help from the Holy Spirit, to preserve their message.

The New Testament has much to say about the Old Testament. Between direct quotations and obvious allusions, the Old Testament makes up about 10% of the New Testament.[23] This is not by accident. There is a clear correlation and storyline that these two reveal together. To divorce one from the other is to take away a part of the information that God is conveying to us. The New Testament writers understood this. They were not going to make claims that God himself did not reveal either in the pages of the Old Testament, or in the teachings of Jesus. As a matter of fact, the most notable Old Testament references come in the teachings of Jesus Christ himself.

It's important to notice that Jesus spoke of the people, events, and teachings as though they were factual, historical, and authoritative. For example, he spoke of Abraham (John 8:33-58), Isaac and Jacob (Matt. 8:11), David (Matt. 12:3; Luke 20:41-44), Solomon (Matt. 6:29), and others as though they were people who really existed. He spoke of Moses's encounter with God at the burning bush as a real event (Mark 12:26) and commanded that they follow his teaching (Matt. 8:4). He also compares the events of his death and resurrection to Jonah (Matt. 12:39-41) and his final return to the flood of Noah (Luke 17:24-26). He also made the blatant statement that "Scripture cannot be broken" when rebuking an angry mob (John 10:35).

Jesus clearly was not afraid to speak about the truth of the Old Testament without any stipulations or qualifications. To Jesus, the Old Testament isn't filled with cute fairytales and fables—it's filled with truth. It's interesting to notice that one of Jesus's common rebukes goes something like this: "Haven't you read the Scriptures?" It's so obvious that God spoke through the Scriptures that he wonders aloud if doubters had read it at all.

As Jesus taught the Old Testament, while building the foundation for the New Testament with his own teachings, his apostles were taking note. It is safe to compare the apostles and other writers of the New Testament to the prophets of the Old Testament. In the same way, the apostles were chosen and given a message from the Lord to take to the world. Mark Roberts says that "early Christians believed all these things to be true about Jesus' words. Thus they had every reason to pass on the sayings of Jesus accurately."[24] Further, Simon Gathercole points out that "Jesus says and does things that not only overlap with what God in the Old Testament says and does," but that he "says and does things that are privileges *uniquely* of the God of Israel."[25]

In a sense, Jesus is saying, "Not only is the Old Testament true, but I wrote it. And what I'm saying now is more of it." These New Testament accounts of his teachings were written soon after the events in some cases, or appeared in near-immediate written form in letters to churches. They knew more Scripture was being communicated and it needed to be written down.

In regards to the New Testament, there are a two particularly important passages to consider concerning the authority of Scripture. Possibly the most quoted verse when speaking about the trustworthiness of Scripture is 2 Timothy 3:16: "All Scripture is breathed out by God and profitable for teaching, for reproof, for correction, and for training in righteousness." Scripture is viewed as God's actual breath, and God does not lie (Num. 23:19; Tit. 1:2; Heb. 6:18). The very thing that brought the universe into existence (Heb. 11:3) and gave Adam life (Gen. 2:7) is delivered to us in the form of the Bible.[26]

It's also encouraging that Peter refers to Paul's letters as Scripture. After encouraging his readers to heed the words of Paul, he warns that some might try to harmfully twist Paul's letters "as they do other Scriptures" (2 Pet. 3:16). To Peter, not only are Paul's letters authoritative Scripture, but it would be dangerous to alter them in any way.

DELIGHTING IN GOD'S TRUTH

The authors of both the Old and New Testaments were not shy about the authority of what they wrote, and we should have the same boldness. They knew that God had spoken and that it was important, so they made sure that others were given access to it. This should cause us to rejoice in the goodness of God for giving us a treasure chest of truth about himself, and we should be thankful that he carried these people along by the Holy Spirit to produce reliable manuscripts that we can trust.

As Christians, we can read the Bible with the expectation that it is not only an account of God's words, but that the Holy Spirit will reveal its truth and use it to change us (John 14:26; 1 Cor. 2:12-13). Remember what our Lord said in John 17:17: "Sanctify them in the truth, your word is truth." The Bible is filled stories, but they are not static. The Word of God is living, active, and armed like an atomic bomb of grace to change our lives for God's glory and our joy (Heb. 4:12). Come to the Bible not to just learn the data, facts, and figures, but to behold the Prince of Peace, the King of Kings, the Word made flesh (John 1:14). Come to the Bible because Jesus invites you to come and sit awhile.

Don't treat the Bible like a fact book, a kind of God-ordained Book of World Records. Isn't that how many view the Bible? It's no wonder many find dread instead of delight when it comes to sitting down with the Scriptures. Far too many Christians treat the Bible like a heavenly Google—you only go to it when you need something. "Where is that verse on _____?" "What does the Bible say about _____?" That's not totally wrong, but it's also not the total purpose of God's book.

His book exists to show you who God is, and we see Jesus as the cog in the story. Jesus said so himself. Jesus and many other authors of the New Testament tell us that the Bible is indeed about him. Jesus told a group of religious men known as the Pharisees, "You search the Scriptures because you think that in them you have eternal life; and it is they that bear witness about me" (John 5:39). Every Christian should have this goal for their life: Don't read the Bible like the Pharisees; read the Bible like the apostles and authors of the New Testament. Our theology of the Scriptures should be rooted in our Christ.

Paul tells us that once we are made new in Christ, the veil is lifted and we can see the glory of Christ and be transformed. "Yes, to this day whenever Moses is read a veil lies over their hearts. But when one turns to the Lord, the veil is removed ... And we all, with unveiled face, beholding the glory of the Lord, are being transformed into the same image from one degree of glory to another" (2 Cor. 3:15-16, 18). He told his disciples in Luke 24 that the Scriptures were written about him, from the beginning of Genesis to the end of Revelation.

Your Bible is alive. Look at it. It sits there rumbling. Growling. Don't be shy. Don't stay behind the yellow line; get close to the roar of the super-natural pages.

Our Bible is living and active because Jesus is living and active (Heb. 4:12-13). It really is super-natural. The Word is most certainly alive, not like a puppy or houseplant—provide it moderate at-tention and you'll derive pleasure from keeping it around. It doesn't eat or drink, require walks, or rest. Rather, the Bible *itself* is food. The Bible takes *us* on walks, and brings us rest. The Bible rever-berates with the power of God (Rom. 1:16; 1 Cor. 1:18; 1 Thess. 1:5). The words that created Neptune are from the same source as the words on the pages of your Bible: God.

No other book packs this kind of clean, organ-ic, pure, sustainable, and multi-generational pow-er. From Adam and Abraham to you and me, the Word of God keeps going, breathing, and making dead things come to life. Souls are made alive and saints are revived by the Word of Life. "Lazarus, come forth" (John 11:43). Remember that? Raw resurrection power from the lips of God. The Spirit flies behind every word, breathing on us, wafting the aroma of Christ into our nostrils, that we may live again—that maybe, just maybe, our groggy eyes will see the glory of Christ (2 Cor. 3:18).

Are you down? No vitality? Worn out? Drop the energy drink and dive into the Word of Life. Keep trying to get run over by the power by the Spirit as you dart through the city blocks and paragraphs, alley-ways and allegories, skyscrapers and prophesies, and meander through it verse-by-verse. Keep traveling. Stay the course. And before you know it, you'll sound like Peter: "Lord, to whom shall we go? You have the words of eternal life" (John 6:68).

Jesus has ordained that we live by every word from cover to cover. "Man shall not live by bread alone, but by every word that comes from the mouth of God" (Matt. 4:4). It is this inspired, God-breathed Word that we read, ingest, and devour for our hope, growth, and confidence. As we will see in the next chapter, our salvation story is a story spanning all of Scripture. Jesus molds us into his image, revealing to us his glory, using his Word and his Spirit (2 Tim. 3:16; Titus 2:11-12). So, in faith, take up and read–taste and see that your Lord is good (Ps. 34:8).

DISCUSSION AND REFLECTION

1. What role does Scripture play in your life?

2. Before reading this chapter, why would you have said you read the Bible? Did your reason change after reading this chapter?

3. How does our understanding of Scripture impact our devotion to God?

4. In what way does Scripture's authority encourage us to share the gospel with others?

3
THE STORY OF REDEMPTION: SIN AND THE GOSPEL

There are many questions these days about our universe. Did galaxies, planets, and stars appear out of nowhere? Did anything exist before our universe? What about the first living organisms? Did humans evolve from monkeys? Is there a purpose for our lives? The list goes on.

Modern scientists have, in a sense, cornered the market when it comes to claiming to have the answers to these questions. While scientists will mostly admit that they cannot explain how the universe initially formed, many today agree that like some sort of intergalactic firecracker on the 4th of July, a "big bang" caused an immediate creation of living organisms. From there, scientists explain that these organisms either evolved into other species or subspecies, adapted to their surroundings, or eventually ceased to exist.

While scientists speculate on how everything came to be, they aren't answering the deeper question: Why did everything come to be? And more pointedly—why am I here?

As Christians, Scripture is our ultimate authority. And the Bible answers life's major questions. Science is not the enemy, but it doesn't give us the final answer.

The first book of the Bible, Genesis, describes the most trustworthy explanation of how and why we're here. Keep in mind, the Genesis account is not an overly-detailed, second-by-second explanation of all that occurred. It's not a science book that attempts to give a formula for every question that ever needed an answer. There are questions left unanswered in the text, but we must not let curiosity cloud our understanding of what God has clearly decided to show us.

Everything starts with God. Not Adam and Eve. Not animals and plants. Not the moon and the stars. Genesis 1–2 is showing us that humans, seahorses, roses, blue jays, and galaxies all find themselves under the category of being created by God. We are all under his power. We are introduced to the historical moments in which God designed existence as we know it, and this is something that should create awe in our hearts and minds. So based on what God has revealed to us, let's answer the question: What happened in the beginning?

IN THE BEGINNING

We know for sure that God created all that exists because Scripture says as much (John 1:3).

In the first chapter of Genesis, we see that God created the physical reality in which we live. He formed the planet earth, stars, light and darkness, land and sea, plants, animals, birds, fish, and everything in between. Then, God creates the first human "in his image." This means that this man, named Adam, would reflect God as his representative in this new world. He would reflect God's authority in how he took care of God's creation, and he would live forever in harmony with God. Contrary to the scientific theory that humans evolved from apes; we were created from dust, not King Kong. Our lungs were jumpstarted by God's breath, not as a continuation from a previous life as a monkey. Scripture describes mankind as the pinnacle of God's creation and the only being living in real relationship with him. After all was said and done, "God saw all that he had made and it was very good" (Gen. 1:31).

God placed Adam in paradise, a place called Eden, and gave him the keys to creation. Adam was given the privilege of taking care of all that God made, and his only limitation was to refrain from eating fruit from the "tree of the knowledge of good and evil" (Gen. 2:9). This restriction was not a silly rule created by God for his own entertainment so he could watch Adam squirm with temptation; rather, it seems that God was showing him what it looked like to tangibly trust him. The tree was a constant reminder of faith. By not eating from this tree, Adam showed that he was confident that God's commands were good and trustworthy.

Though everything else in creation had its own counterpart, Adam did not. He was alone, but not lonely, for he was with God in the Garden of Eden. But this is the first time God says that something is "not good" (Gen. 2:18). Did God goof up here? Never. God is working his plan. God is setting the stage for a gift of grace—the first marriage.

God remedies the situation, as only God can, by creating a complementary person for Adam. Taken out of Adam's rib, God created a woman named Eve. She was so perfect for Adam that he delightfully and poetically proclaims, "This at last is the bone of my bones and flesh of my flesh" (Gen. 2:23). He was complete. As picture-perfect companions, they lived in Eden "naked and unashamed" (Gen 2:25). In other words, Adam and Eve were completely innocent and full of joy, walking in flawless relationship with one another and with their God.

They are told "be fruitful and multiply" God's image, his kingdom reign, to the ends of the earth. It was the first Great Commission: Go and make worshipers of God. But it didn't last.

PARADISE LOST

If you only spend a few moments watching or reading the news, it is obvious that the world no longer resembles the peaceful reality of Eden. Death, destruction, famine, hatred, greed, and brokenness are not the exception today. They are the norm. They are so common that these things are described as inevitable or expected. No one expects life to be perfect or to go on forever—but we know, in our core, it should not be this way. Doesn't it all seem out of place and unnatural? Guess what? It is.

How did everything get this way? We find our answer in Genesis 3. Satan, the enemy of God disguised as a serpent, challenges God's command to stay away from the tree. He asks Eve, "Did God actually say, 'You shall not eat of any tree in the garden'?" (Gen. 3:1). We see later in the Bible that Satan likes to twist God's words (Matt. 4:1-11). He convinces Adam and Eve that God is a liar, and that God is holding out on them. He convinced them that God doesn't want them to be like him, so he tells them to stay away from the tree (Gen. 3:3-6). After being tempted by Satan, our ancient parents ate the fruit, immediately noticed that they were naked, and hid from God. They were ashamed.

They were self-conscious. They were scared. They had disobeyed their Creator, and they knew it. They handed over their God-given responsibility to God's great enemy. This was the first sin.

Sin can be described as "anything (whether in thoughts, actions, or attitudes) that does not express or conform to the holy character of God as expressed in his moral law."[27] Sin is rebellion against God, first and foremost. Some say that to sin means to "miss the mark." When we sin, we don't just miss the mark—we point the bow in the other direction and shoot into the sky. Sin causes us to "fall short of the glory of God" (Rom. 3:23) and leaves us under God's wrath (Rom. 1:18). It doesn't just cause division between people or cause us a little more trouble that we'd like. Sin brings division between people and life, and because of sin, death is now something we all must deal with. The gut-wrenching stories we see on the news every night are an integral part of living in a world infected by sin.

Sin also brings division between God and people. We see this immediately when Adam and Eve were taken out of the Garden of Eden because of their sin against God. Their perfect relationship with him was damaged from then on out (Gen. 3:16-19). This left mankind freefalling toward utter destruction. But God wasn't through yet, as we will see.

Not only were Adam and Eve punished for their sin, but the consequences of their rule-breaking affects every person born afterward. They passed the nature of sin to their children, and it's been passed along ever since. The Apostle Paul says that "just as sin came into the world through one man, and death through sin, and so death spread to all menbecause all sinned" and that "one trespassed to condemnation for all men" (Rom. 5:12-19). Sin runs in the family.

Sin is a disease that makes the bubonic plague seem like a common cold. Sin is deadly, in every sense of the word. It's the real Black Death. It brings not only physical death, but also spiritual death. Our bodies are buried in the ground, but even worse, souls without Christ are banished to hell, a place of torment and never-ending separation from God (Matt. 25:46; Jude 1:7; Rev. 21:8). As we will see later, physical death can and will be defeated, but spiritual death lasts into eternity. Adam and Eve, and all of us, were made to live forever with God. Now, we all are sentenced to death from the very start apart from his forgiveness (Rom. 3:9-18; 6:23).

We need to be delivered from sin and its effects. The Apostle Paul felt the soul-crushing burden of sin, and he wanted to be done with it. "Wretched man that I am! Who will deliver me from this body of death? Thanks be to God through Jesus Christ our Lord" (Rom. 7:23–25). Deliverance from sin, the undoing of Satan's work in the Garden of Eden, is found in the person and work of Jesus Christ. As John says, "The reason the Son of God appeared was to destroy the works of the devil" (1 John 3:8).

Simply put, Jesus came to conquer Satan and restore the world to its rightful King.

REDEMPTION COME

Jesus is the most important person that lived, lives, and ever will live. He sits alive today in the heavenly places as the Cosmic King, inviting sinners to repent and place their complete trust in him for the forgiveness of sins and the hope of eternal life. It's all about Jesus. This Galilean carpenter is the hope of the world. The entire plan of God (Gal. 4:4-5), the whole swing of the Scriptures (John 5:39), and the sum of human history all lands squarely—like nails ripping through flesh, bone, and wood—on Jesus (Eph. 1:10). All things belong to Jesus, and all things were created by Jesus (Col. 1:15). And right now, all things are held together by Jesus, from Haley's Comet to the micro-skin-flake falling from your fingernail. Jesus is in control. "In him all things hold together" (Col. 1:17) and, "he upholds the universe by the word of his power" (Heb. 1:3).

Is that your Christ? Do you have towering thoughts about the Lord Jesus, or are they reduced to a first-century Israelite who had a knack for healing and preaching? "Who is Jesus?" isn't the mega-stumper question on the SAT. This isn't the dreaded pop quiz question that you *know* you studied but can't remember. This is eternity. This is your life now and your life to come.

In the Gospel of Matthew, Jesus asked his disciples this very question. "Now when Jesus came into the district of Caesarea Philippi, he asked his disciples, 'Who do people say that the Son of Man is?' And they said, 'Some say John the Baptist, others say Elijah, and others Jeremiah or one of the prophets.' He said to them, 'But who do you say that I am?'"(Matt. 16:13–15). Is Jesus just a teacher? Is Jesus just a healer? A popular prophet? Captain of the fib team? Peter answered, "You are the Christ, the Son of the living

God" (Matt. 16:16). So, what then? Who is this man?

Like the great C. S. Lewis said, "Socrates did not claim to be Zeus, nor the Buddha to be Bramah, nor Mohammed to be Allah. That sort of claim occurs only in Our Lord and in admitted quacks or lunatics. I agree that we don't 'demand crystal perfection in other men', nor do we find it. But if there is one Man in whom we do find it, and if that one Man also claims to be more than man, what then?"[28]

The quest for the biblical Jesus is the most important quest you'll ever take.

JESUS IS GOD AND MAN

Jesus, according to Peter, is the Christ, the Messiah, the long anticipated Satan-crushing Son of God (Gen. 3:15), born of a virgin (Isa. 7:14; Matt. 1:22-23), who gave his life as a ransom for many (Mark 10:45). Being the Son of God doesn't make

Jesus any less God than God the Father or God the Holy Spirit. Jesus is full-strength divinity. When Jesus, the eternal Son of God, became a man, in what is known as the Incarnation, he didn't lose his Godness. He added sinless humanity to his perfect deity. He is God and man. We saw this in the chapter on the Trinity, but it's worth revisiting.

Jesus said he is God. Father Abraham looked forward to worshiping Jesus (John 8:58). In John 10:27–30, Jesus says that he grants eternal life to sinners, and that he and the Father are one. The crowd understood exactly what Jesus was trying to get across. "The Jews picked up stones again to stone him" (John 10:31). Why? "For blasphemy," they say, "because you, being a man, make yourself God" (John 10:33). Jesus said he is God. Weather patterns and raging storm cells obeyed Jesus (Matt. 8:24). Defunct cellular structures submitted to the lordship of Jesus. "And great crowds came to him, bringing with them the lame, the blind, the crippled, the mute, and many others, and they put them at his feet, and he healed them" (Matt. 15:30). And even the dark demonic powers, knew Jesus is God. "And demons also came out of many, crying, 'You are the Son of God!' But he rebuked them and would not allow them to speak, because they knew that he was the Christ" (Luke 4:41). And so did his followers. Wonderfully, the Word of God provides seven texts, from four different authors, that undeniably refer to Jesus as God, the word *theos* in Greek.

The Apostle John:

- In the beginning was the Word, and the Word was with God, and the Word was God (*theos*). (John 1:1)
- No one has ever seen God; the only God (*theos*), who is at the Father's side, he has made him known. (John 1:18)
- Thomas answered him, "My Lord and my God (*theos*)! (John 20:28)

The Apostle Paul:

- To them belong the patriarchs, and from their race, according to the flesh, is the Christ, who is God (*theos*) over all, blessed forever. Amen. (Rom. 9:5)
- Waiting for our blessed hope, the appearing of the glory of our great God (*theos*) and Savior Jesus Christ. (Titus 2:13)

The Apostle Peter:

- Simeon Peter, a servant and apostle of Jesus Christ, to those who have obtained a faith of equal standing with ours by the righteousness of our God (*theos*) and Savior Jesus Christ. (2 Pet. 1:1)

The Writer of Hebrews:

- But of the Son he says, "Your throne, O God (*theos*), is forever and ever, the scepter of uprightness is the scepter of your kingdom. (Heb. 1:8)

John, Thomas, Paul, and Peter—men who all believed and understood the Old Testament's predictions—look at Jesus and say, "Theos! He is God!" We are not in danger of having too high and awesome thoughts of Jesus. The treacherous cliff is the low thoughts. Wrong thoughts. In the glorious wisdom of God, Jesus is 100% God and 100% man. Jesus is a real-live man. He was naturally born in Bethlehem, in a supernatural way to Mary the virgin—exempting him from the line of Adam's sin. Jesus ate, drank, walked, smiled, slept, and wept. His skin was ripped apart and he bled all over Jerusalem—from the lashings on his back, a crown of thorns on his head, and nails and a spear piercing his body, all resulting in his death.

The Jesus we read of in the New Testament was no mirage, ghost, or transcendental Spirit hologram—Jesus is human and God. "His deity is demonstrated by his own claims supported by his divine attributes and miraculous activities. His humanity is demonstrated by the virgin birth and his human attributes, activities, relationships, trials, and temptations."[29] Jesus's awesome miracles—walking on water, healing various sickness, exponentially providing food for the crowds, raising people from the dead, being raised from the dead himself—reveal his divine power over all. His miracles are not baptized party tricks. They are neon signs or flare guns announcing that the kingdom of God had arrived.

And it's still here because Jesus is still alive.

Jesus breathed and Jesus *breathes*. Jesus put his feet on Jerusalem soil and Jesus sits on a throne in heaven. Jesus was. Jesus *is*. Jesus is to come. There are past events with Jesus—but Jesus isn't locked down in the past. He is wonderfully present. He is with us till end of the age and the dawn of the new one (Matt. 28:20). The cross of Christ, though it killed him, didn't end him. He died and he rose again, heart and lungs pumping, brain firing on all cylinders, for the justification, the pardoning of sinners. "It will be counted to us who believe in him who raised from the dead Jesus our Lord, who was delivered up for our trespasses and raised for our justification" (Rom. 4:24–25).

JESUS'S CROSS AND EMPTY TOMB

No one will ever do anything greater than Jesus. He gave up his life on a Roman death device, a wooden cross outside of Jerusalem, on a public hill, so that he could pay for the sins of all who would believe in him for salvation—to bring us back to that Eden-like relationship with God (1 Pet. 3:18). The beloved Son of God was given to us, and gave up his life for us, so that whoever believes would be freed from sin, Satan, and death, and be given eternal life in him (John 3:16). Eden was lost, but it's coming back. What made Eden great was unhindered, unfiltered relationship with the Holy God. And God sent his Son to redeem and restore all that Adam and Eve and their children lost in the Garden of Eden. Paradise is being restored by the Lord Jesus. But it came at great cost.

God is omni-just. He can never fudge on his justice. Sins, the cosmic crimes that sinners commit against God, must be dealt with. All humanity sits under the curse of sin, in line for the wrath of God, "but God, being rich in mercy, because of the great love with which he loved us, even when we were dead in our trespasses, made us alive together with Christ—by grace you have been saved— and raised us up with him and seated us with him in the heavenly places in Christ Jesus, so that in the coming ages he might show the immeasurable riches of his grace in kindness toward us in Christ Jesus. For by grace you have been saved through faith. And this is not your own doing; it is the gift of God, not a result of works, so that no one may boast" (Eph. 2:4–9). This awesome gift came wrapped in flesh, decorated with blood. God's great love for us is found not in a cute note, but in a bloody crime scene and an executioner's hill. Jesus hung on that cross, next to two criminals, while completely innocent. He hung there, not for his crimes, but for ours. Not his sins, but ours. Jesus died in our place under the mighty wrath of God. As we are told in Isaiah 53:5-10:

> But he was pierced for our transgressions; he was crushed for our iniquities; upon him was the chastisement that brought us peace, and with his wounds we are healed. All we like sheep have gone astray; we have turned—every one—to his own way; and the LORD has laid on him the iniquity of us all. He was oppressed, and he was afflicted, yet he opened not his mouth; like a lamb that is led to the slaughter, and like a sheep that before its shearers is silent, so he opened not his mouth. By oppression and judgment he was taken away; and as for his generation, who considered that he was cut off out of the land of the living,

stricken for the transgression of my people?
And they made his grave with the wicked
and with a rich man in his death, although
he had done no violence, and there was no
deceit in his mouth. Yet it was the will of the
LORD to crush him; he has put him to grief.

JESUS DIED IN OUR PLACE

When Jesus hung on the cross, he made a beautiful statement: "It is finished" (John 19:30). He died in *our place, for us,* and for *his* glory. Jesus is our substitute who atoned, paid for, our sins—till the last drop. "He himself *bore our sins* in his body on the tree, that we might die to sin and live to righteousness. By his wounds you have been healed" (1 Pet. 2:24). "I am writing to you, little children, because your sins are forgiven *for his name's sake*" (1 John 2:12).

Jesus wasn't overcome by an angry mob of Jewish leaders and Roman soldiers because he was some weakling. When we look at the cross, Jesus isn't looking for our pity. He's looking for absolute, unceasing praise. Jesus joyfully gave up his life, "for the joy that was set before him endured the cross" (Heb. 12:2). He didn't wake up with cancer one morning. He didn't get into a multi-camel collision on the Galilean Freeway. For Jesus to be a substituting savior, he willingly gave up his breath, and he would take it up again. Jesus said about his life, "No one takes it from me, but I lay it down of my own accord. I have authority to lay it down, and I have authority to take it up again. This charge I have received from my Father" (John 10:18).

Good Friday was mapped out by the triune God from ages past. The night that Jesus was arrested he told the disciples, "For the Son of Man goes as it has been *determined*" (Luke 22:22). And after Jesus rose from the dead, he met up with some disciples and told them, "'These are my words that

I spoke to you while I was still with you, that *everything written about me in the Law of Moses and the Prophets and the Psalms must be fulfilled.'* Then he opened their minds to understand the Scriptures, and said to them, 'Thus it is written, that the Christ should suffer and on the third day rise from the dead'" (Luke 24:44–46).

In Acts chapter 2, when Peter gave his Spirit-powered sermon, he said concerning the cross of Christ, "This Jesus, *delivered up according to the definite plan and foreknowledge of God*, you crucified and killed by the hands of lawless men. God raised him up, loosing the pangs of death, because it was not possible for him to be held by it" (Acts 2:23–24). Jesus "gave himself for our sins to deliver us from the present evil age, *according to the will of our God and Father*" (Gal. 1:4). God's plans didn't get derailed when Jesus took the nails—it was being fulfilled. Every thorn on his brow, every splinter on his back, and the puddle of blood at the soldier's feet—it all happened, like sovereign clockwork, according to God's gracious blueprint to redeem sinners. Jesus hung on the cross, not as some kind of motivational poster, but as the Savior who was literally paying for our sins and giving us his righteousness, his perfect standing with God the Father.

What happened at Calvary is what many theologians have called the Great Exchange. Jesus took our sin and he gave us his righteousness. "For our sake he made him to be sin who knew no sin, so that in him we might become the righteousness of God" (2 Cor. 5:21). Jesus became sin. He took on our sins and the identities of sin—adulterer, thief, liar, swindler, gossiper, and alcoholic. He took them all so that we could become all that he is in the heavenly places. Jesus is our brother (Heb. 2:11); we are no longer orphans in the universe, we are in God's family because of big brother. "See what kind of love the Father has given to us, that we should be called children of God; and so we are." (1 John 3:1). As Martin Luther said, "Therefore everything which Christ has is ours, graciously bestowed on us unworthy me out of God's sheer mercy."[30]

All that belongs to Jesus, he shares with us. "And if children, then heirs – heirs of God and fellow heirs with Christ" (Rom. 8:17). These gifts of grace, these gospel glories, came at a high cost. Jesus took on a curse so that we could take on blessing. "Christ redeemed us from the curse of the law by becoming a curse for us—for it is written, 'Cursed is everyone who is hanged on a tree'" (Gal. 3:13). Jesus became our curse, the curse of Adam's back in Genesis. "But of the tree of the knowledge of good and evil you shall not eat, for in the day that you eat of it *you shall surely die*" (Gen. 2:17). Jesus paid the penalty of Adam's sin on a tree. And now, the day that we eat of the fruit of Calvary's tree, his flesh and blood—when we put our faith in Christ the Lord—we shall surely live in him and with him.

JESUS ROSE FOR US

Jesus died so that we could die with him. By faith in his name, we've been united in his death-payment for our sins so that we don't have to pay for them. Everyone dies for their sins. We either die on the cross with Christ or we die for them ourselves and pay for them eternally under the wrath of God.

Gloriously, Jesus is alive. And Jesus rose so that we could live with him. By faith in his name, we've been united in his resurrection like his. "For if we have been united with him in a death like his, we shall certainly be united with him in a resurrection like his" (Rom. 6:5).

Jesus's body kicked back to life on that Easter morning (Matt. 28:5–10; Mark 16:6–8; Luke 24:5–9; John 20:11–18). It was a spiritual resurrection—and a physical resurrection. His amino acids began to flutter about, his brain stem booted up, and his heart began to pump. Jesus is alive. In his rising, he overcame death for us. Death no longer has a claim on the children of the King. Death's sting has been plucked. Since Jesus breathes, death is like a housefly to the saints. It's annoying, but it cannot ruin the Christian. As Paul proclaims, "O death, where is your victory? O death, where is your sting?" (1 Cor. 15:55). It's been left in the ground, along with all our sins, and now there is no condemnation for those who are in Christ Jesus (Rom. 8:1).

More than that, his resurrection was the introduction of something even more amazing—his resurrection body was and is the first of its kind. When others were raised from the dead, they died again. Jesus's body, on the other hand, walked out the grave perfect and new, a body just like the one we will receive when we are resurrected one day. A body that won't fall apart and sputter out like an old pickup truck. We are ruin-proof, spiritually now and physically on that Last Day, because Jesus's body didn't get whittled down to dust and came back better than any other before it. We too will be risen from the dead, in the twinkling of an eye. A trumpet will blare and we will be given glorious bodies like the risen Christ and we will dwell with him for 20 billion years and then some (1 Cor. 15:52; 1 Thess. 4:16–18).

THE CRUCIFIED LIFE

While the Calvary-event happened one weekend in Jerusalem, we are to deny our own desires and pick up our cross daily and follow Jesus (Mark 8:34). Crucifixion happened *for* us and *to* us. And now we view our lives, our identities—the totality of all that we are—as being "in Christ." Now, our greatest accomplishment is something we didn't do, but rather something that's been done for us and in us. We boast in Jesus's cross. Paul reminds us, "But far be it from me to boast except in the cross of our Lord Jesus Christ, by which the world has been crucified to me, and I to the world. For neither circumcision counts for anything, nor un-circumcision, but a new creation" (Gal. 6:14–15). What is most significant about our lives is that we have been crucified with Christ.

Paul gives us the vision of the crucified life in Galatians. His words here have been used by the Holy Spirit to change lives in innumerable ways. We pray the Lord uses these words in high-watt-age ways. May this be your vision, your hope, your comfort in life and in death: "I have been crucified with Christ. It is no longer I who live, but Christ who lives in me. And the life I now live in the flesh I live by faith in the Son of God, who loved me and gave himself for me" (Gal. 2:20).

Though Jesus is the centerpiece of the Scrip-ture's story of redemption, we see the triune God at work. The Father sends the Son, the Son sends the Spirit, the triune God sends us. The Trinity gives salvation its shape. And the only response is worship and obedience.

DISCUSSION AND REFLECTION

1. Why is it important to understand the entire story of Scripture and not just bits and pieces?
2. How does Jesus being God and man impact our salvation?
3. In what ways do the Father, Son, and Holy Spirit each play a role in our salvation?
4. Why should the redemption story compel us to share the gospel with others?

4
ALREADY AND NOT YET: THE CHURCH AND ETERNITY

It's the end of the world as we know it. Seriously. But this is no reason to panic, worry, or stock your pantry with jugs of water and pallets of astronaut ice cream.

Sadly, when some Christians begin to study Eschatology–the doctrine of the last things–they tend to get antsy, frazzled, angry at the world, or flat out paranoid. And there are other Christians who refuse to offer no more than a shoulder shrug when it comes to the end times. They don't care about seminary debates—premillennialism, amillennialism, postmillennialism, pre-tribulational raptures, etc. They'll say, "I'm a panmillennialist. I believe it'll all pan out." Others simply don't care at all: "God will sort it out when I die."

Others take the lead, confident—positive!—that their prediction is true. They make the charts our nonchalant friends ignore. They write books like *88 Reasons the World Will End in 1988*. Of course, it never happens. We know the verse they seem to ignore: "But concerning that day and hour no one knows, not even the angels of heaven, nor the Son, but the Father only" (Matt. 24:36). These predictors change their formulas over and over again, never willing to admit that they're simply wrong. They just write another book. Start another speaking tour. Name the next president or pope the Antichrist.

But all of these postures are wrong. Eschatology isn't meant to freak us out or check us out; according to the Apostle Paul, it's meant to impact us right now. The Thessalonian church is wondering about the return of Jesus, the resurrection to come, and what is going to happen to the church members who have already died. Paul writes:

> *"For the Lord himself will descend from heaven with a cry of command, with the voice of an archangel, and with the sound of the trumpet of God. And the dead in Christ will rise first. Then we who are alive, who are left, will be caught up together with them in the clouds to meet the Lord in the air, and so we will always be with the Lord. Therefore encourage one another with these words."* (1 Thess. 4:16-18)

What does Paul think the doctrine of Christ's return, the resurrection, and eternal life with Jesus should foster among Christians? Encouragement. Empowerment. Whatever your position on eschatology is (or isn't), if it doesn't foster mutual encouragement of other Christians or empower you to live an eternity-driven life, you haven't understood your eschatology. In fact, as we will see, the end of all things is the greatest hope the world has. If eschatology is not encouraging and life-redirecting, it's not biblical.

As we continue this final chapter on the last things, we won't be diving deep into what typically divides us. No disaster forecasts. No meteors or ice ages or zombie apocalypses. No charts telling us who will be left behind and when.

Our aim is that you'll finish this chapter feeling encouraged, excited, and eager for the return of King Jesus. We pray that you'll have joy in the hope of unending life with him and all those from Adam who call upon his name. We long to see you live in ways you never have with purpose you've never experienced.

So let's talk about the most underrated encouragement of all: death.

DEATH IS OVERCOME

We are all going to die.

That statement isn't meant to be grim, morbid, or cavalier. It's realistic. We are all careening toward our last breath in these fallen bodies. As we saw earlier in this book, death is a reality. It's inescapable. Running from death is like a turtle running from a cheetah. No chance. But in the end, that's good news.

Christians have no need to fear death because we are going to be raised from the dead, joining Jesus in a resurrection like his. Paul reminds the Roman church:

> "For if we have been united with him in a death like his, we shall certainly be united with him in a resurrection like his. We know that our old self was crucified with him in order that the body of sin might be brought to nothing, so that we would no longer be enslaved to sin. For

> *one who has died has been set free from sin.*
> *Now if we have died with Christ, we believe*
> *that we will also live with him. We know that*
> *Christ, being raised from the dead, will never*
> *die again; death no longer has dominion over*
> *him. For the death he died he died to sin, once*
> *for all, but the life he lives he lives to God. So*
> *you also must consider yourselves dead to sin*
> *and alive to God in Christ Jesus." (Rom. 6:5-11)*

Translation: You've already died spiritually. And through Christ, you've already been made alive spiritually. That's where it begins: here and now. If you're reading this, you haven't died physically, though. Not yet. But you will.

And because of Jesus's bodily resurrection, we don't look at death with fear, but in faith that we too will rise. Death isn't the final nail in the coffin. There is a glorious eternity on the other side of a non-beating heart because Christ conquered death on its home court. One day there won't be enough nails in the coffin to hold you in.

That first Easter Sunday was a game-changer. The resurrection of Jesus—the death of his death—is so altering to reality that when Christians die, the Bible refuses to stoop down and pander to death's scare tactics. Instead, God uses a simple metaphor to describe a Christian's death—we've fallen asleep. Our bodies are at rest, covered in a blanket of dirt, but the alarm clock of the Lord's trumpet will sound and we will have new, glorified, and eternity-ready bodies. Jesus is the first fruits, the first harvest of the Resurrection, and another wave of reconstituted and remade bones and organs will rise (1 Cor. 15:20). We will live in the New Earth with King Jesus and all those from every corner of the planet who called upon the name of the Lord.

> "But we do not want you to be uninformed,
> brothers, about those who are asleep, that
> you may not grieve as others do who have

> *no hope. For since we believe that Jesus*
> *died and rose again, even so, through*
> *Jesus, God will bring with him those who*
> *have fallen asleep."* (1 Thess. 4:13-14)

Grieving over someone's death is biblical, Christ-like (John 11:35). We often say, "Death is a natural part of life." It's actually the opposite–death is entirely unnatural. We weren't created to die, and we aren't destined to stay dead. That's why Jesus mourned over Lazarus's death, but also pumped blood back through his veins. That resuscitation was a picture of the resurrection to come. So we don't grieve as though all is lost. Since Jesus rose from the dead, we are filled with a gospel-ratified battle cry, "O death, where is your victory? O death, where is your sting?" (1 Cor. 15:55).

When we see death the way Scripture describes it, we are able to look beyond a flat lining heart and hope in an impending horizon of eternal life with our triune God. But what happens after we do flat line, when the doctors deliver the news to our loved ones that we won't be waking up again this side of eternity?

WHAT HAPPENS WHEN WE DIE?

"If we live, we live for the Lord; and if we die, we die for the Lord. Therefore, whether we live or die, we belong to the Lord. Christ died and came to life for this: that he might rule over both the dead and the living." (Rom. 14:8-9)

God is not detached from death; he's right in the midst of it. Whether we live or die, he's there; he's in control. The eternal Son of God, Jesus, experienced death for us. And like his death on the cross, whatever happens is for our good and his glory.

Paul can call death "gain" (Phil. 1:21) because to be with Christ is far better than any bucket list (Phil. 1:23). "Death is a passage to glory," says

Thomas Manton, "It shall not separate us from Christ, but join us to him."[31] Is this how we view death? Your death? How you view death says a lot about you. Spurgeon prods and pokes us when he says, "I take it that our view of our own death is one of the readiest tokens by which we may judge of our own spiritual condition."[32] If you have a paralyzing fear of death, you are living as one who has no hope. You are living with a bad eschatology. If you are worried you'll be bored in eternity (and you feel bad even thinking that), this also reveals an ill-informed eschatology. We are thinking too little of Christ and too much of the things that moth and rust will destroy.

While our bodies are put in the ground, we are long gone. We are in heaven, in paradise, with the Lord (Luke 23:43). When we go the funeral of a believer we hear statements like, "Praise the Lord, Tommy was a Christian." What do we mean, "was"? Tommy still is. He exists in a tsunami of glory in the presence of King Jesus. When we see a body at a funeral, we should be, as John Phillips translates 2 Corinthians 5:8, "so sure of this that we would really rather be 'away' from the body and be 'at home' with the Lord."

Christians who believe in the sovereign goodness of God realize no one dies "too soon." It may be too soon from our vantage point, but not from God's. There is no alternate universe wherein that person was alive a little longer. Instead, he or she was rushed quickly into the presence of the Creator, right on time. "What if" doesn't exist. God has already numbered, logged, and catalogued the day our birth certificates would get dabbed with inky baby feet, and the day our death certificates will get their last ink dot from the printer. "Your eyes saw my unformed substance; in your book were written, every one of them, the days that were formed for me, when as yet there was none of them" (Ps. 139:16). For Christians, this gives us new eyes to see death. We can look beyond the sadness and look for a serene cityscape designed by God himself.

THIS WORLD IS OUR HOME—FOREVER

You may have heard the old hymn lyrics, "This would is not my home. I'm just passing through." While this sounds sweet, even hopeful, it isn't true. We were put on this earth to rule as God's image-bearers, stewarding creation and spreading image-bearers to every corner of the planet (Genesis 1-2). This world *is* our home. And it will continue to be.

We're always trying to leave this world. But God the Son came into this world and will come back to redeem this world. We're not abandoned. God's not pulling the plug on this planet. Randy Alcorn says, "If God were to end history and reign forever in a distant Heaven, Earth would be remembered as a graveyard of sin and failure."[33] God doesn't fail. Whatever we think about *why* sin entered the world, we know one thing: God isn't leaving it that way. He has a plan, and he's sticking to it.

Scripture tells us that God is going to make a New Earth. It will be familiar, interesting, awe-inspiring, and new. You'll recognize the feel of Saint Augustine grass between your toes, but it will feel... perfect. You'll enjoy the smell of the sweetest Guatemalan coffee you've ever encountered. You'll talk and laugh and sing with your brothers and sisters who've been redeemed by the blood of the Lamb. Here's how Revelation describes the New Earth:

> "Then the angel showed me the river of the water of life, bright as crystal, flowing from the throne of God and of the Lamb through the middle of the street of the city; also, on either side of the river, the tree of life with its twelve kinds of fruit, yielding its fruit each month. The leaves of the tree were for the healing of the nations. No longer will there be anything accursed, but the throne of God and of the Lamb will be in it, and his servants will

worship him. They will see his face, and his name will be on their foreheads. And night will be no more. They will need no light of lamp or sun, for the Lord God will be their light, and they will reign forever and ever." (Rev. 22:1-5)

Eat your heart out, George Orwell.

Notice that John mentions "the tree of life." We've seen this before in Scripture, but it's often overlooked. The tree of life makes its debut all the way back in Genesis. The tree of life was in the Garden with Adam and Eve. It was the *other* tree— the one we ignore because of the tree that led to sin and death, "the tree of the knowledge of good and evil."

When sin led to eviction from the Garden, Adam and Eve were separated from God. That's the most crucial consequence. But packing their bags and leaving the Garden also meant separation from the tree of life. God "stationed the cherubim and the flaming sword which turned every direction to guard the way to the tree of life" (Gen. 3:24). No life only means one thing—death.

But on the New Earth, humanity is given access to the tree of life once more. Through Christ, the cherubim are given an eternal vacation from tree-guarding. They have been discharged from their task of wielding swords to keep us from the tree (Gen. 3:24) because Jesus went up on a tree and under the sword, dying and rising, so we can enjoy eternal life. He crushed sin, and no sin means no separation from the tree of life.

Heaven is not our eternal home. We may be there for a time, in the presence of God, but he has more for us. We don't spend forever in the clouds with God in some fanciful dream world, shedding our earth-suits, leaving this world an empty shell. Rather, heaven and earth will come together in one physical, concrete place. We'll experience the answer, the *promise*, of the Lord's Prayer, "Your kingdom come, your will be done, on earth as it is in heaven" (Matt. 6:10). Heaven and earth meet in an orderly and glorious way. The charter of Eden will be reestablished in the "New Jerusalem." We will take dominion of earth as co-heirs with Jesus. We won't sit on clouds playing harps. We won't grow angels' wings like some sort of *X-Men* character. We won't disappear into a prayer closet where it's just "me and Jesus." How boring! Why have streets of gold if we aren't going to use them? Why have a mansion if we won't have block parties and throw the football around? They are pointless if we are cooped up in an eternal church service.

The reason so many of us feel unsettled about worship in the New Earth is because we are confused about worship here and now. We forget that worship is more than a song. We lose sight of the fact that whether we are eating or drinking, or whatever we do, it can be done for the glory of God (1 Cor. 10:31). True worship is glorifying God in all of life—to the perimeters and edges of life. Sunday hymns aren't the only means of glorifying God. The risen Christ demands that our whole self be devoted to him. Food, leisure, money, and work are aligned to glorifying Jesus Christ. And this is what we will live on the New Earth. We will live as Jesus lived for us.

We will sing—and it will be like we've never sung before because we will see King Jesus, and singing will no longer seem difficult. But remember, if we are going to join Jesus is in a resurrection like his, what is the resurrected Jesus like? What do we see Jesus doing after his resurrection?

Was Jesus in a 24/7-singing-mode? Did he write first-century CCM hits for three decades? Nope. He walked, talked, and had shoreside cook-outs (John 21:9–14). If we are going to be made like Jesus, we are also going to act like Jesus. We will be glorified men and women, and all of our eating, drinking, and whatever else we'll do on the New Earth, will glorify the triune God.

If you want to understand what the New Earth will be like, here's what you can do: Look around you. It will be like this—but perfect, purged from sin and its stains. We will walk out of the grave like Jesus did. We will be whole, body and soul, the way we were always meant to be. As C. S. Lewis says, we will have a new model of the body to cruise around in. "As we grow older, we become like old cars—more and more repairs and replacements are necessary. We must just look forward to the fine new machines (latest Resurrection model) which are waiting for us, we hope, in the Divine garage!"[34]

When we rise again, we will take the most natural breath of air we've ever inhaled. We'll be home, but it will be *Extreme Makeover: Home Edition* on steroids. Death and pain and suffering will be no more. Sin will be conquered. Satan and his minions will be stamped out (Rev. 20:10). We will feast on the fruit of the tree of life right here in the same little neck of the Milky Way.

LIVING NOW FOR THE DAY TO COME

You may be thinking, "Great! I can't wait for that day. But what about now?" It's a good question—one we should all ask. Our lives now matter for eternity.

"Do good works now and prepare yourself for that day" or "just believe in God and do your best" is an easy answer. And in some sense, it's correct. The Bible hints at that, actually (Rom. 2:5-6; 2 Tim. 4:8). But that's not all. Again—how boring!

Our lives have a purpose now. Every tick of the second hand is a tick closer to Jesus's return. We don't know if Jesus will return in our lifetime. Even Jesus said that he didn't know (Matt. 24:36). This is why we should avoid Last Day predictions like a daily special on expired hot dogs. But we should also be fully aware that it could happen any minute. We should realize we have hope in Christ beyond this life, and we have a city to look forward to, who's architect and builder is God (Heb. 11:10).

This sense of urgency—excitement!—should propel us toward two immediate actions. First, we should be living as though the time has already come. This means living obediently to God's call to holiness, living like we will when sin and death are no more (1 Cor. 15:34). We've been made alive, to live as those who proclaim the death of sin in our lives. We have a new Master of whom all worship is worthy now and forever.

Second, we should be on God's mission of redemption by showing and proclaiming the good news of eternity with him to those around us. Perhaps your neighbor, your co-worker, your family member, or your dearest friend has heard the gospel but has never heard about the all-encompassing hope of the future. "Your sins are forgiven now if you believe on the name of Jesus" is true and a place to start, of course. But there is even more—a beautiful, joyful, redeemed new world where we not only fall on our knees in worship, but we also recline at the table with Jesus in fellowship for eternity.

You really don't need a bucket list. You want to snorkel in Fiji? You can do that in the New Earth. As a co-heir, you will *own* Fiji. You'll have eternity to enjoy the New Earth and beyond. Maybe we'll charter a trip with friends to Moon or Mars. Why not? We'll have billions, trillions, and quintillions of years to enjoy all that our God has made.

You won't be disappointed in eternity; life on the New Earth will astound you over and over. For example, you can enjoy zoos today but there won't be any in eternity. No cages. No fear between us and lions, tigers, and silverback gorillas. No more *When Animals Attack* reruns.

When you are enjoying God's glory on the New Earth, you won't lean over and say to Moses after coffee, "You know what, Mo? I wish I had bought that Tesla back on the Old Earth. Such a great car, you know?" Just won't happen. What we need today is a gospel-minded bucket list. In eternity, you won't be able to travel to Thailand and tell unreached peoples about Jesus. You won't be able to give your money to pro-life movements. You won't be able to evangelize your friends and family members, urging them to look to Jesus. That's for now. Today. Right now. This is the mindset we need today.

Since there is a resurrection to come, life today is recalibrated. Looking to the resurrection lifts you out of the pit of pursuing pleasures that are irrelevant in ten billion years—or even ten minutes. When the angels rolled back the stone on Jesus's tomb, all of our idols we've propped up are now destabilized by the power of the resurrection. So what if you don't have the house you've always wanted? He's gone to prepare a place for you. So what you don't make the money you crave? The resurrection to come reveals that money doesn't make your world go 'round, Jesus does. Since Jesus is alive, you and I are co-heirs of the universe; we aren't controlled by what moths and rust will destroy.

We live best on this earth when we live towards the New Earth. Our calling in the present is to see the world through futuristic lenses. We have seen the final score before the game is over. If we get knocked down, if the scoreboard looks hopeless because it seems we've lost too much ground, we remember that we will be victors in the end. We are encouraged and empowered by the hope that all things will be made new.

HELL IS REAL, BUT SO IS HOPE

Hell is always difficult to talk about. Books about hell don't typically top bestseller lists. But it is a sobering reality for Christians, and one we must confront with both reverence and hope. When sin entered the world, God didn't turn a blind eye. In his justice and mercy, he's provided the Savior. Don't ever believe a pastor who avoids talking about hell. That pastor is not loving you well. Jesus says, "The angels will come out and separate the evil from the righteous and throw them into the fiery furnace. In that place there will be weeping and gnashing of teeth" (Matt 13:49–50). Jesus didn't avoid hell, and neither should we.

As we consider the glories of the New Earth, we can't ignore the horrors of hell. It is appointed for all to die and appear before judgment (Heb. 9:27). Revelation reminds us:

> "Then I saw a great white throne and him who was seated on it. From his presence earth and sky fled away, and no place was found for them. And I saw the dead, great and small, standing before the throne, and books were opened. Then another book was opened, which is the book of life. And the dead were judged by what was written in the books, according to what they had done. And the sea gave up the dead who were in it, Death and Hades gave up the dead who were in them, and they were judged, each one of them, according to what they had done. Then Death and Hades were

thrown into the lake of fire. This is the second death, the lake of fire. And if anyone's name was not found written in the book of life, he was thrown into the lake of fire." (Rev. 20:11–15)

When Judgment Day arrives, Christians—because of Christ's righteousness—will enter into the Master's joy, and unbelievers will be judged according to their sin, and they will suffer the consequences. As those who have been saved from the wrath of God, because of faith in Christ alone—who suffered for our sin on the cross—we will enjoy eternity with God. We cannot ignore or deny that some people will also spend eternity apart from the grace of God, under his wrath. All of the common grace that unbelievers experience now will be done away with, and they will eternally perish under God's holy wrath for their sin, "'where the worm does not die and the fire is not quenched.' For everyone will be salted with fire" (Mark 9:48–49). Hell doesn't belong to Satan; it's not his to rule. He's not laid up in hell in a fire-mansion with a pitchfork, smiling and laughing. Satan will suffer under the wrath of God, suffering in that very place forever (Rev. 20:10).

Our hearts should break. While our eternal life excites us, the eternal wrath that awaits unbelievers should move us to evangelize. There is hope in Christ. Everlasting forgiveness is found with Jesus, by faith alone in his death for our sins and in his resurrection from the dead.

The church, Christ's body, is called to live now in the light of the future. We live as though we jumped into a DeLorean and traveled from eternity to the present. Our lives are meant to reflect what they will be in the age to come. Life on the New Earth, were God's kingdom reigns forever, has begun through the Spirit living in us.

The triune mission carried out in the person of Jesus is our hope. We are forgiven because of Jesus. We are made new because of Jesus. We will be resurrected because of Jesus. We will live on the

New Earth because of Jesus. We'll live faithful on this earth, waiting for the clouds to roll back with Jesus sitting on a white horse, ready to make temporary war in exchange for eternal peace. Let's look to him. As James Hamilton says:

> We need the grace of Jesus. He was faithful unto death, and God raised him from the dead. We must follow him in faithfulness, and we need his grace to do so. Jesus was raised by the glory of the Father, and if we follow in his footsteps by grace through faith, we too will be raised to reign with him.[35]

It's the end of the world as we know it, and we feel fine. In fact, we remember, "He who testifies to these things says, 'Surely I am coming soon.' Amen. Come, Lord Jesus! The grace of the Lord Jesus be with all. Amen" (Rev. 22:20–21).

Amen.

DISCUSSION AND REFLECTION

1. How would you have described the end times before reading this chapter? How about now?

2. How does understanding the end times impact our lives today?

3. In what ways do the truths about the New Earth impact our devotion to God?

4. How do the end times influence why and how we share the gospel with others?

NOTES

[1] A. W. Tozer, *The Knowledge of the Holy* (New York, NY: HarperCollins, 1961), 1.

[2] C. S. Lewis, *Mere Christianity* (New York, NY: HarperCollins, 2001), 154.

[3] Kevin J. Vanhoozer, *The Drama of Doctrine*: A *Canonical Linguistic Approach to Christian Theology* (Louisville, KY: Westminster John Knox Press, 2005), 16.

[4] Ibid., 57.

[5] Michael F. Bird, *Evangelical Theology*: A *Biblical and Systematic Introduction*, (Grand Rapids, MI: Zondervan, 2013), 41.

[6] David Clark, *To Know and Love God* (Wheaton, IL: Crossway, 2003), 245.

[7] According to Box Office Mojo. [Accessed on

April 20, 2015, from http://www.boxofficemojo. com/seasonal/?view=releasedate&yr=2012&season=Summer]

[8] Philip Ryken and Michael LeFebvre, *Our Triune God: Living in the Love of the Three-in-One* (Wheaton, IL: Crossway, 2011), 13.

[9] Ryken and LeFebvre, *Our Triune God*, 74.

[10] Bruce Ware, *Father, Son, and Holy Spirit: Relationships, Roles, and Relevance* (Wheaton, IL: Crossway, 2005), 61.

[11] Francis Chan, *Forgotten God: Reversing Our Tragic Neglect of the Holy Spirit* (Colorado Springs, CO: David C. Cook, 2009), 18.

[12] Alister McGrath, *Understanding the Trinity* (Grand Rapids, MI: Zondervan, 1988), 142.

[13] Leland Ryken, "How We Got the Best-Selling Book of All Time," *The Wall Street Journal* 26 August 2011. [Accessed on April 29, 2015, from

http://online.wsj.com/article/SB10001424053 111903918104576502782310557332.html]

[14] "Chicago Statement on Biblical Inerrancy,"

Journal of the Evangelical Theological Society Volume 21, No. 4 (December 1978): 289.

[15] Wayne Grudem, *Systematic Theology: An Introduction to Biblical Doctrine* (Grand Rapids, MI: Zondervan Academic, 1994), 91.

[16] "The Great Isaiah Scroll," Google Cultural Institute, [http://dss.collections.imj.org.il/isaiah], Accessed May 5, 2015.

[17] Garry K. Brantley, "The Dead Sea Scrolls and Biblical Integrity," 1995, Apologetics Press, [https://www.apologeticspress.org/apcontent.aspx?category=13&article=357], Accessed May 5, 2015.

[18] J. Ed Komoszewski, M. James Sawyer, Daniel B. Wallace, *Reinventing Jesus: How Contemporary Skeptics Miss the Real Jesus and Mislead Popular Culture* (Grand Rapids, MI: Kregel, 2006), 72.

[19] Matt Slick, "Manuscript evidence for superior New Testament reliability," Christian Apologetics and Research Ministry, [http://carm.org/manuscript-evidence], Accessed May 5, 2015.

[20] Michael F. Bird, *The Gospel of the Lord: How the Early Church Wrote the Story of Jesus* (Grand Rapids, MI: Eerdmans, 2014), 95-105.

[21] J. I. Packer, *"Fundamentalism" and the Word of God: Some Evangelical Principles* (Grand Rapids, MI: Eerdmans, 1958), 89.

[22] Willem A. VanGemeren, *Interpreting the Prophetic Word: An Introduction to the Prophetic Literature of the Old Testament* (Grand Rapids, MI: Zondervan, 1990), 33.

[23] René Pasche, *The Inspiration and Authority of Scripture* (Chicago, IL: Moody, 1969), 97.

[24] Mark D. Roberts, *Can We Trust the Gospels?: Investigating the Reliability of Matthew, Mark, Luke, and John* (Wheaton, IL: Crossway, 2007), 75.

[25] Simon Gathercole, "What Did the First Christians Think about Jesus?" in *How God Became Jesus: The Real Origins of Belief in Jesus' Divine Nature*, ed. Michael F. Bird (Grand Rapids, MI: Zondervan, 2014), 99.

[26] For more on this idea, see: Carl F. H. Hen-

ry, *God, Revelation, and Authority*, vol. 4, *God Who Speaks and Shows: Fifteen Theses, Part Three* (Waco, TX: Word, 1979), 129-31.

[27] Erik Thoennes, "Biblical Doctrine, An Overview," in *The ESV Study Bible* (Wheaton, IL: Crossway, 2008), 2530.

[28] C. S. Lewis, *The Collected Letters of C.S. Lewis, Volume 3* (New York: HarperCollins, 2007), 1377-1378.

[29] Gregg R. Allison, *Historical Theology: An Introduction to Christian Doctrine* (Grand Rapids, MI: Zondervan, 2011), 365.

[30] Timothy F. Lull, *Martin Luther's Basic Theological Writings* (Minneapolis: Augsburg Fortress, 2012), 120.

[31] Thomas Manton, *The Complete Works of Thomas Manton*, vol. 12 (London: James Nisbet & Co., 1873), 419.

[32] C. H. Spurgeon, *The New Park Street Pulpit Sermons*, vol. 5 (London: Passmore & Alabaster, 1859), 393.

[33] Randy Alcorn, *Heaven* (Carol Stream, IL: Tyndale House, 2004), 137.

[34] C. S. Lewis, *The Collected Letters of C. S. Lewis*, ed. Walter Hooper, vol. 3 (New York: HarperCollins ebooks, 2004–2007), 975.

[35] James M. Hamilton Jr., *Revelation: The Spirit Speaks to the Churches* (Wheaton, IL: Crossway, 2012), 419.

Made in the USA
Columbia, SC
24 June 2022

62187693R00090